VOLUME 1

Color Like Crazy!

KALEIDOSCOPE MANDALA
DESIGNS
BY MARY TANANA

Color Like Crazy! Kaleidoscope Mandala Designs, Volume 1
© 2015 Mary Tanana

WWW.MARYTANANA.COM
© MARY TANANA 2015
GROOVITY
PRESS

For Mom and Dad...

With special thanks....

To my fabulous friends, a very talented and fierce group of international designers, also known as "The Honey Badgers". I couldn't have gotten to this point without your support and guidance.

I also have to thank my longtime friends, J Bruce Jones and Louise Miller, who convinced me to recognize the power of coloring! Thanks so much!

The illustrations in this coloring book are intricate and challenging. The best media to use are colored pencils, gel pens, and fine tip markers. Try placing a blank sheet of paper between the pages to prevent any bleed through.

Happy Coloring!

color like crazy!

Meet the Artist, Mary Tanana!

At a very early age, I was doing all kinds of crafts. I did embroidery, needlepoint, counted cross-stitch, quilling, crochet, starting at age 6. My parents were so wonderful, they gave into my every craft whim! Coming from a family of engineers, I am so thankful they supported me! In college I studied Fashion Illustration, and along the way, I discovered Surface Pattern Design, and completely fell in love with it! I took as many courses as I could fit into my schedule, but left Syracuse University with a BFA in Fashion Illustration. Incredibly, I landed a job as a jewelry designer in a company that photo-etched gold and silver jewelry. I was so excited to have any kind of design job, and the bonus was that It was about drawing intricate designs that were pierced and etched to create patterns in fine metals. Later, I was excited to interpret my design skills into gem, diamond and bridal jewelry. I had many opportunities to travel globally and lived in Hong Kong where I led a large group of designers and frequently commuted into China. This was a huge evolution in my career and my vision. International cultures opened my eyes to diversity and opportunity.

But after almost 20 years I decided I needed a change in my life and some extra help in order to return to my creative roots in pattern making. With everything being done digitally, I enrolled in as many courses as I could find, some online and others at important Universities like the rhode island school of design. I rediscovered my passion and love of surface pattern design and have immersed my work in this medium.

My design style is usually expressed as complicated patterns work and line drawings. I begin with hand sketched layouts on paper which I scan into an adobe program which allows me to add fine line work. I create multiple layers which is what makes my designs intricate. I'm fascinated with Henna Designs from India. Folk Art form the Ukraine, Russia and Poland. My design friends say that they can recognize my style instantly and that is professional praise that I am flattered by. I've traveled extensively and always take a lot of photograph's to perpetuate the memories. I am inspired to translate the diversity of art, architecture and landscape that I have been blessed to connect with. I always try to translate a form into something fresh. I am an avid gardener and find Mother Nature to be some of my most important inspiration especially the colors and textures that project in flowers, shrubs and trees.

CONNECT WITH ME!

I WOULD LOVE TO SEE HOW YOU USE MY BOOK
AND ILLUSTRATIONS!!

PLEASE USE THE HASHTAG

#COLORLIKECRAZY

ON INSTAGRAM, FACEBOOK, PINTEREST, AND TWITTER

MARY TANANA

FOLLOW ME!

HTTP://INSTAGRAM.COM/GROOVITY
HTTPS://TWITTER.COM/MJTDESIGNS
HTTP://PINTEREST.COM/GROOVITY/
HTTPS://WWW.ETSY.COM/SHOP/GROOVITY
HTTPS://WWW.FACEBOOK.COM/GROOVITYDESIGNS
BLOG: HTTP://GROOVITYDESIGNS.COM/

Please check out my other coloring book titles!

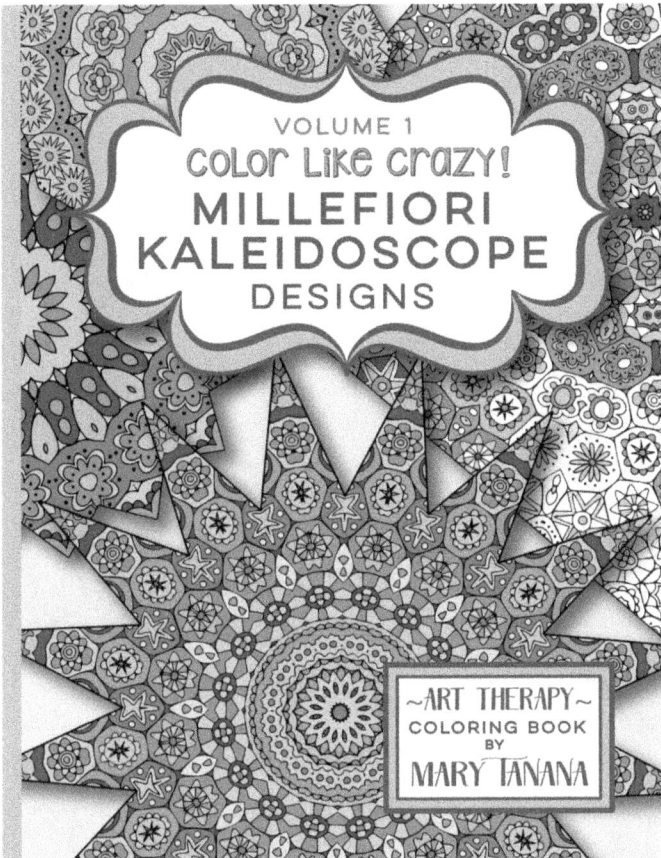

VOLUME 1
color Like crazy!
MILLEFIORI KALEIDOSCOPE DESIGNS
~ART THERAPY~
COLORING BOOK
BY
MARY TANANA

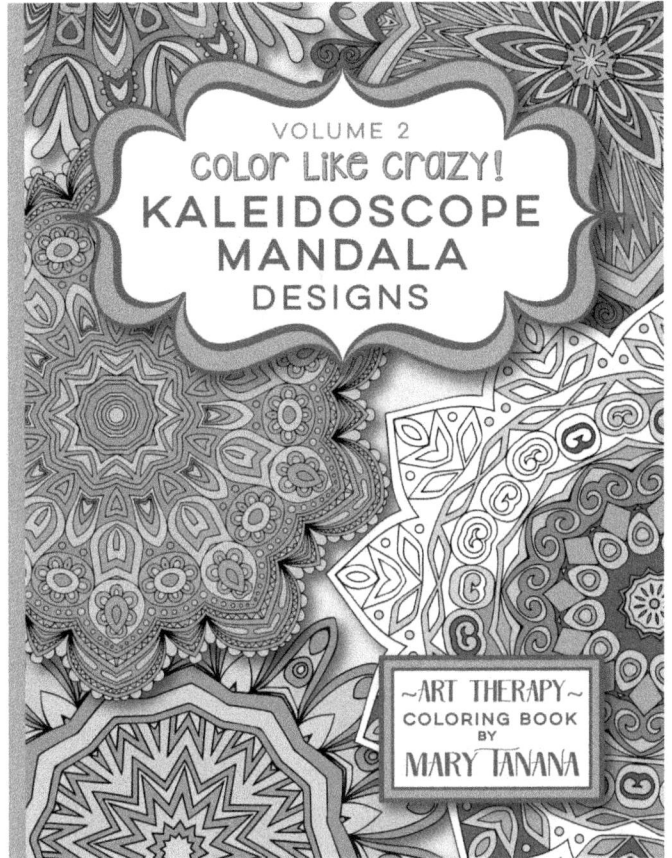

VOLUME 2
color Like crazy!
KALEIDOSCOPE MANDALA DESIGNS
~ART THERAPY~
COLORING BOOK
BY
MARY TANANA

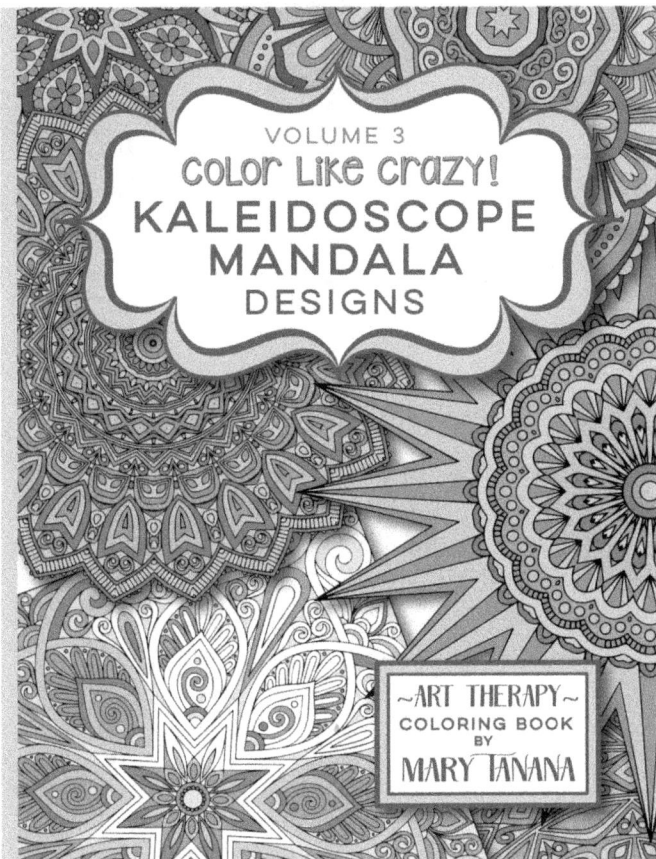

VOLUME 3
color Like crazy!
KALEIDOSCOPE MANDALA DESIGNS
~ART THERAPY~
COLORING BOOK
BY
MARY TANANA

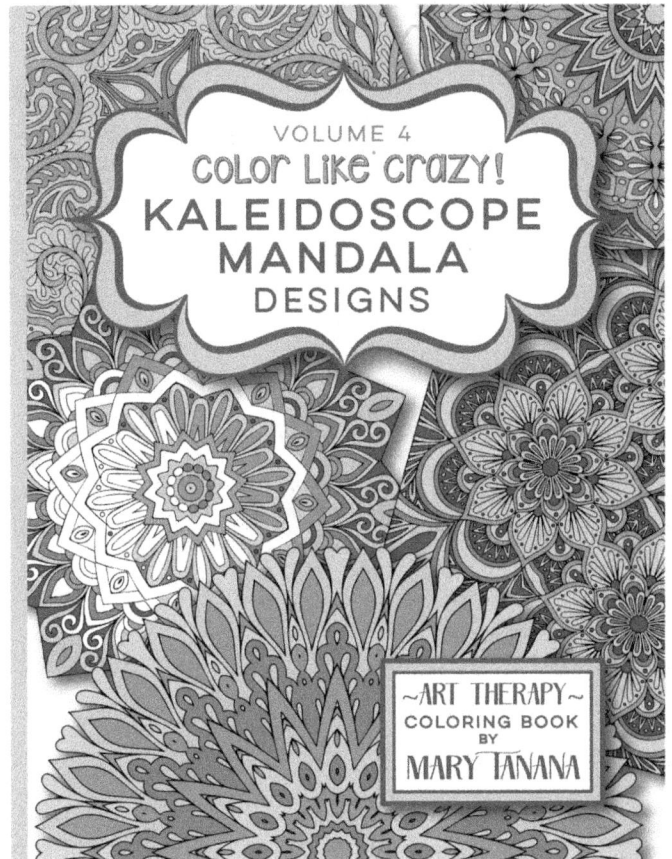

VOLUME 4
color Like crazy!
KALEIDOSCOPE MANDALA DESIGNS
~ART THERAPY~
COLORING BOOK
BY
MARY TANANA

GROOVITY

...WHERE CREATIVITY GROWS...

WWW.GROOVITYDESIGNS.COM

www.ingramcontent.com/pod-product-compliance
Lightning Source LLC
Chambersburg PA
CBHW081213020426
42331CB00012B/3018